TUDOR	STUART	GEORGIAN	VICTORIAN	MODERN TIMES
1485-1603	1603-1714	1714-1837	1837-1901	1902-NOW

children's HISTORY of SHEFFIELD

Written by
Ann Wright

HOMETOWN WORLD

How well do you know your town?

Have you ever wondered what it would have been like living in Sheffield when the Romans arrived? What about working in the dusty grinding workshop at Shepherd Wheel? This book will uncover the important and exciting things that happened in your town.

Want to hear the other good bits? You will love this book! Some rather brainy folk have worked on it to make sure it's fun and informative. So what are you waiting for? Peel back the pages and be amazed at what happened in Sheffield.

THE FACTS

Timeline shows which period (dates and people) each spread is talking about

The Romans Arrive!

Marius is on guard beside the Roman camp. His legs are tired after the long march north. Behind him, camp fires flicker and soldiers settle in their leather tents. Across the river, there is a Brigante fort. Marius has heard the Brigantes are fierce! He clutches his javelin, hoping he will not need it. Then he hears two soldiers talking nearby. Their leaders have made peace with the Brigantes. They will be looking for a good spot to build a fort of their own! Marius smiles. That means no more marching!

We can spot invaders coming from Wincobank Hill. But we're no match for the Roman army.

Sheffield has five rivers flowing through and around the town. Sheaf, Loxley, Porter brook and Rivelin

A Powerful Tribe

In AD 43 when the Romans arrived in Britain, Sheffield was not a town, but there were people living here. They were part of a large Celtic tribe, called the Brigantes, who ruled over much of the area now known as Yorkshire. The Brigantes were a warlike people, ruled by a powerful queen called Cartimandua.

At Wincobank there was an Iron Age hill fort near the River Don. This was the very edge of Brigantes land. The fort had a wall 5.5 metres thick, made of stone, rubble and timber. This was surrounded by a deep ditch. The Brigantes probably used the fort to protect the people who lived on the farms nearby. From the fort high on the hill, they could see all around.

You can still see the shape of the fort's rampart and ditch on Wincobank Hill, near Meadowhall shopping centre.

A Fort Across the River

It was AD 54 before Roman soldiers reached the Brigantes border. They were called the Fourth Cohort of Gauls. By then Queen Cartimandua had become a friend of the Romans and they allowed her to carry on ruling her people.

The Roman army built a wooden fort of their own across the river Don, to protect the edge of their land. There were eight hundred soldiers at the new fort, and they had money to spend! Traders arrived to sell food from the farms and local crafts made of metal and pottery. Shops and houses were built near the fort and a small town known as a vicus grew up.

The Romans built their fort at Templeborough between Sheffield and Rotherham.

A New Peace

But things were not peaceful for long! The Brigantes fought amongst themselves and by AD 69 Cartimandua was no longer queen. A new leader, Venutius, took charge and started a rebellion against the Romans. The friendship between the Brigantes and the Romans was over. More Roman soldiers arrived and many battles were fought between AD 71 and AD 85 until the Romans were in charge of the north.

The Roman fort was rebuilt in stone around AD 100. The Romans brought new foods and built new roads. Retired Roman soldiers began to settle on farms around Sheffield. At last, the Romans and the Brigantes all learned to live together in peace.

A steelworks was built on top of Templeborough Roman Fort. Today, it's the Magna Science Adventure Centre.

SPOT THIS!
The Romans believed in many gods. Vulcan was a blacksmith and the god of fire. His statue of Vulcan is on top of Sheffield Town Hall.

AD 43 ROMANS ARRIVE IN BRITAIN...AD 54 TEMPLEBOROUGH FORT BUILT...

...AD 69 BRIGANTES TRIBE REBELS...AD 100 ROMANS REBUILD FORT...

Clear informative text

Hometown facts to amaze you!

'Spot this!' game with hints on something to find in your town

THE EVIDENCE

Floriana is a ten year-old girl who might have lived in a Roman villa in Sheffield in about AD 140. Her father is a retired Roman soldier who has been given some land to farm. In this imagined story she tells us about a trip to the market with their crops.

I'm going to save some coins and bury them in a secret place so no one can steal them.

We had good crops of leeks, broad beans, parsnips, turnips and carrots this year. Father decided to sell some at the market outside the Roman fort. He promised to take me, but first I had to do my work! Today, I got up before dawn and quickly ate some plums and bread for breakfast. After that, I fed the ducks and chickens. Brr, it was cold outside! Then I helped Mother knead the dough to make bread. Mother had put hot charcoal on the stove, so the kitchen was warm and cosy. It smelled of the mint, parsley, rosemary and thyme we have hanging up to dry. When it was light we set off for market with a cart full of vegetables. Our mare, Claudia, knows her own way there! Father spent all day gossiping with his old friends from the fort. For midday meal he bought oysters and sausages from the food stalls, but I do not like oysters so he ate them all! He gave me some money and I bought my favourite things to take home. Dates and honey!

this jar is called an amphora. Romans used these for transporting foods such as olive oil, wine or a sauce called garum. Garum was made from fish and fish guts. It was very smelly to make!

The Romans called the British 'butter eaters' because they ate butter instead of olive oil!

this diploma from AD 124 was found at Stannington. It belonged to a soldier who may have been given land there after serving 25 years in the Roman army.

How do we know?

We know about the local tribes because a Roman historian, called Tacitus, wrote about the Brigantes tribe. He tells us that Queen Cartimandua was 'a member of a powerful family who ruled the Brigantes'.

Archaeologists digging at Wincobank fort discovered a wall which had once been burnt down! They also found Roman pottery in the ditch, and a Roman coin nearby. This could mean the Brigantes still had a fort when the Romans were there. Quern-stones for grinding corn were found too, so there may have been farming settlements around the fort.

Memorial stones found at Templeborough fort record that the Fourth Cohort of Gauls were there. Parts of old buildings, coins and pottery were found outside the fort. These were probably remains of a vicus.

Roman military diplomas found under a stone on farmland at Stannington in 1761 are a clue that retired Roman soldiers may have farmed there.

The Romans built a fort upriver from modern Sheffield.

Intriguing old photos

Go back in time to read what it was like for children growing up in Sheffield

Each period in the book ends with a summary explaining how we know about the past

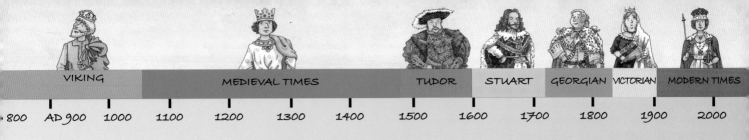

Contents

The Romans Arrive!

Marius is on guard beside the Roman camp. His legs are tired after the long march north. Behind him, camp fires flicker and soldiers settle in their leather tents. Across the river, there is a Brigante fort. Marius has heard the Brigantes are fierce! He clutches his javelin, hoping he will not need it. Then he hears two soldiers talking nearby. Their leaders have made peace with the Brigantes. They will be looking for a good spot to build a fort of their own! Marius smiles. That means no more marching!

Sheffield has five rivers flowing through and around it – the Don, Sheaf, Loxley, Porter Brook and Rivelin.

We can spot invaders coming from Wincobank Hill. But we're no match for the Roman army.

A Powerful Tribe

In AD 43 when the Romans arrived in Britain, Sheffield was not a town, but there were people living here. They were part of a large Celtic tribe, called the Brigantes, who ruled over much of the area now known as Yorkshire. The Brigantes were a warlike people, ruled by a powerful queen called Cartimandua.

At Wincobank there was an Iron Age hill fort near the River Don. This was the very edge of Brigantes land. The fort had a wall 5.5 metres thick, made of stone, rubble and timber. This was surrounded by a deep ditch. The Brigantes probably used the fort to protect the people who lived on the farms nearby. From the fort high on the hill, they could see all around.

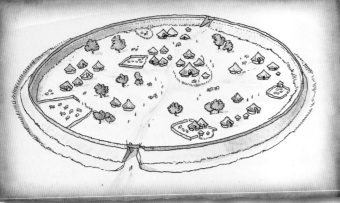

You can still see the shape of the fort's rampart and ditch on Wincobank Hill, near Meadowhall shopping centre.

TUDOR
1485-1603

STUART
1603-1714

GEORGIAN
1714-1837

VICTORIAN
1837-1901

MODERN
TIMES
1902-NOW

A Fort Across the River

It was AD 54 before Roman soldiers reached the Brigantes border. They were called the Fourth Cohort of Gauls. By then Queen Cartimandua had become a friend of the Romans and they allowed her to carry on ruling her people.

The Roman army built a wooden fort of their own across the river Don, to protect the edge of their land. There were eight hundred soldiers at the new fort, and they had money to spend! Traders arrived to sell food from the farms and local crafts made of metal and pottery. Shops and houses were built near the fort and a small town known as a vicus grew up.

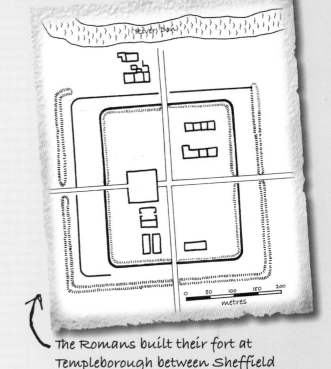

The Romans built their fort at Templeborough between Sheffield and Rotherham.

A steelworks was built on top of Templeborough Roman Fort. Today, it's the Magna Science Adventure Centre.

A New Peace

But things were not peaceful for long! The Brigantes fought amongst themselves and by AD 69 Cartimandua was no longer queen. A new leader, Venutius, took charge and started a rebellion against the Romans. The friendship between the Brigantes and the Romans was over. More Roman soldiers arrived and many battles were fought between AD 71 and AD 85 until the Romans were in charge of the north.

The Roman fort was rebuilt in stone around AD 100. The Romans brought new foods and built new roads. Retired Roman soldiers began to settle on farms around Sheffield. At last, the Romans and the Brigantes all learned to live together in peace.

SPOT THIS!

The Romans believed in many gods. Vulcan was a blacksmith, and the god of fire. This statue of Vulcan is on top of Sheffield Town Hall.

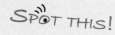

...AD 69 BRIGANTES TRIBE REBELS...AD 100 ROMANS REBUILD FORT...

5

CELT
500 BC

ROMAN
AD 43-410

ANGLO-
SAXON
AD 450-
1066

VIKING
AD 865-
1066

MEDIEV
TIME.
1066
1485

Floriana is a ten year-old girl who might have lived in a Roman villa in Sheffield in about AD 140. Her father is a retired Roman soldier who has been given some land to farm. In this imagined story she tells us about a trip to the market with their crops.

I'm going to save some coins and bury them in a secret place so no one can steal them.

We had good crops of leeks, broad beans, parsnips, turnips and carrots this year. Father decided to sell some at the market outside the Roman fort. He promised to take me, but first I had to do my work! Today, I got up before dawn and quickly ate some plums and bread for breakfast. After that, I fed the ducks and chickens. Brr, it was cold outside! Then I helped Mother knead the dough to make bread. Mother had put hot charcoal on the stove, so the kitchen was warm and cosy. It smelled of the mint, parsley, rosemary and thyme we have hanging up to dry. When it was light we set off for market with a cart full of vegetables. Our mare, Claudia, knows her own way there! Father used to be a soldier, so at the market he spent all day gossiping with his old friends from the fort. For midday meal he bought oysters and sausages from the food stalls, but I do not like oysters so he ate them all! He gave me some money and I bought my favourite things to take home. Dates and honey!

The Romans called the British 'butter eaters' because they ate butter instead of olive oil!

This jar is called an amphora. Romans used these for transporting foods such as olive oil, wine or a sauce called garum. Garum was made from fish and fish guts. It was very smelly to make!

TUDOR
1485-1603

STUART
1603-1714

GEORGIAN
1714-1837

VICTORIAN
1837-1901

MODERN TIMES
1902-NOW

This diploma from AD 124 was found at Stannington. It belonged to a soldier who may have been given land there after serving 25 years in the Roman army.

How do we know?

We know about the local tribes because a Roman historian, called Tacitus, wrote about the Brigantes tribe. He tells us that Queen Cartimandua was 'a member of a powerful family who ruled the Brigantes'.

Archaeologists digging at Wincobank fort discovered a wall which had once been burnt down! They also found Roman pottery in the ditch, and a Roman coin nearby. This could mean the Brigantes still had a fort when the Romans were there. Quern-stones for grinding corn were found too, so there may have been farming settlements around the fort.

Memorial stones found at Templeborough fort record that the Fourth Cohort of Gauls were there. Parts of old buildings, coins and pottery were found outside the fort. These were probably remains of a vicus.

Roman military diplomas found under a stone on farmland at Stannington in 1761 are a clue that retired Roman soldiers may have farmed there.

The Romans built a fort upriver from modern Sheffield.

CELT
500 BC

ROMAN
AD 43-410

ANGLO-
SAXON
AD 450-
1066

VIKING
AD 865-
1066

MEDIEV
TIME.
1066
1485

Two Kings Meet

A cold wind is blowing across the moors.
A shepherd boy hears the thud of many
horses approaching from the north.
His dog barks a warning. It is an army!
They wear large knives and swords and
carry shields. Their helmets and mail
coats gleam in the morning sun. The boy
hides behind a rock, scared. The leader
looks important. Could this be the king
of Northumbria? Then he sees another
army coming from the south. Soon the two
armies will meet. Will there be a battle?

Map of
Angle-Land

A Ruler for England

By AD 410, the Romans had left and the British no longer
had a strong army to protect them. The Angles, Saxons
and Jutes began to arrive from Germany and Denmark.
Over the following centuries, the country was divided
up into many small kingdoms. Each king wanted more
power, so they all fought to make their kingdoms
bigger. The Sheffield area became part of the northern
kingdom of Northumbria. It was ruled by an Anglo-
Saxon King called Eanrad.

Around AD 829, King Egbert of Wessex marched his
army to Dore in Sheffield to conquer King Eanrad's
land. But there was no battle this time. King Eanrad
surrendered, and agreed that King Egbert was now
'Bretwalda' – an Anglo-Saxon word that meant he
was ruler over all.

But King Egbert soon faced a new challenge. There
were terrifying invaders causing trouble. The Vikings!

The map shows Sheffield and the Anglo-
Saxon kingdoms AD 600–900.

Raiders from the Sea!

The Vikings came from Denmark and Norway to raid, trade and seek out new lands to settle. They first attacked in AD 793, stealing from the monasteries in the north. Then, in AD 866 a mighty army of Danish Vikings captured York. They took over Northumbria and within ten years they had shared out the land between them and begun farming. A line was drawn down the country, with the eastern half ruled by the Danes and the western half ruled by the English. The people of Sheffield were in the half now ruled by the Danes! The Danish part of the country became known as the Danelaw. New settlers came to start their own farms and bit by bit everyone began to speak the same language.

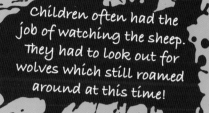

Children often had the job of watching the sheep. They had to look out for wolves which still roamed around at this time!

Dore is the Old English for door. It was the gateway from one Kingdom to another.

SAXON AND VIKING PLACE NAMES

beck	small stream
eccles	church
feld	treeless area
forth	river crossing
ham	homestead
ley	woodland clearing
thorpe	outlying farm

How do we know?

Monks wrote down what happened in England in Anglo-Saxon times. The Anglo-Saxon Chronicle tells us about the Viking invasion and King Egbert.

Place names tell us what it was like to live here. The early Anglo-Saxons lived in a 'feld' beside the the River Sheaf. The words 'Sheaf' and 'feld' were put together, to make Sheffield. So Sheffield means a treeless area beside the river Sheaf.

Part of an Anglo-Saxon stone cross was found in Sheffield.

SPOT THIS!

Can you spot this plaque on Dore village green? It is shaped like a Saxon shield and has the Golden Dragon of Wessex on it.

KING ECGBERT OF WESSEX LED HIS ARMY TO DORE IN THE YEAR A.D 829 AGAINST KING EANRED OF NORTHUMBRIA BY WHOSE SUBMISSION KING ECGBERT BECAME FIRST OVERLORD OF ALL ENGLAND

CELT
500 BC

ROMAN
AD 43-410

ANGLO-
SAXON
AD 450-
1066

VIKING
AD 865-
1066

MEDIEV
TIMES
1066-14

An Important Wedding

The young serving girl is hot and tired. She has been kneading bread and stirring cooking pots all day! The air is full of the smell of roasting beef, goose, pork and venison. It is a feast for Earl Waltheof and his friends. He has arrived at his hall in Sheffield with his new wife, Judith! Everyone is talking about it. Judith is the niece of King William! The king has punished many people in the north for rebelling against him. Perhaps now that his niece is married to Earl Waltheof, the king will be kind to the people of Sheffield.

The new castle had an armoury, a granary, barns, stables and a moat.

Tax records from 1297 tell us the earliest known Sheffield knife-maker was Robert the Cutler.

Rebellion!

By 1066, England was ruled by a Saxon king called Harold. But he was not king for long! William of Normandy invaded with 7,000 men and defeated King Harold's army at Hastings. King Harold was killed by an arrow in the eye. William was crowned king, and became known as William the Conqueror.

At the time, Earl Waltheof was lord of Hallam Manor, which is now part of Sheffield. He promised to obey King William. In return the king allowed Waltheof to keep his lands. He also allowed Waltheof to marry his niece, Judith. But, in 1075, Waltheof joined in a rebellion against William. As punishment, his head was chopped off!

These windows in Sheffield Cathedral show Earl Waltheof and William de Lovetot.

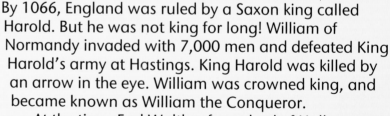

...1075 WALTHEOF REBELS...1270 CASTLE REBUILT IN STONE...

TUDOR
1485-1603

STUART
1603-1714

GEORGIAN
1714-1837

VICTORIAN
1837-1901

MODERN
TIMES
1902-
NOW

The Town Grows

Hallam Manor eventually became the property of a Norman knight named William de Lovetot. He built a castle in about 1100 made of earth and timber. He also built a corn mill on the banks of the River Don.

Around this time, Lady's Bridge was built near the castle making it easier for traders to come to the town. A hospital for sick poor people was built at Spital Hill, and the first parish church was built. The Cathedral now stands on the same spot as the first church. It was an exciting time for Sheffield.

This is what Sheffield Castle may have looked like around 1300.

A New Market!

The castle and lands later passed to a family called de Furnival. When the wooden castle was burnt down in 1266, the de Furnivals replaced it with a massive stone one around 1270. In 1296, Thomas de Furnival was given a Charter by the king. This allowed Sheffield to hold a market every Tuesday, and a three-day fair every year. A year later another charter granted land to people in return for a yearly payment. It also gave the townspeople the right to fine or whip criminals, or put them in the town stocks!

The Domesday book tells us there were 150-200 people living in Sheffield in 1086.

How do we know?

In 1085, King William sent men all over England to write down what land and animals everyone owned. The Domesday book tells us that Waltheof had a hall in Sheffield, known as an Aula.

Archaeologists have unearthed parts of the stone castle, and parts of the wooden castle, which had burned down.

Town records from the time tell us about Thomas de Furnival's charters, and when the bridge was rebuilt. The townsmen paid a stonemason called William Hill nearly £67 to build it.

SPOT THIS!

Lady's Bridge was rebuilt in 1485. Can you spot some of the old stonework?

CELT
500 BC

ROMAN
AD 43-410

ANGLO-
SAXON
AD 450-
1066

VIKING
AD 865-
1066

MEDIEV
TIME
1066
1485

A Royal Plot

It is a cloudy winter's afternoon and the marketplace is busy and noisy. The clatter of hammers rings out from the cutlery workshops. Suddenly a boy runs through the street, shouting. A great procession is coming! The people fall quiet and stand back. They stare as a line of soldiers ride slowly through the streets and into the castle courtyard. With them is a woman in a warm cloak. Someone whispers. Could it be the Scottish Queen who has been plotting against Queen Elizabeth?

They say that Queen Mary's ghost can sometimes be seen in a window of the Turret House!

A Prisoner in Sheffield

In Tudor times, Sheffield castle was owned by George Talbot, Earl of Shrewsbury. Queen Elizabeth I gave him the important job of guarding her cousin, Mary Queen of Scots. Mary was suspected of plotting to claim the English throne. Mary Queen of Scots arrived at Sheffield in November 1570 and was taken to the castle. She did not spend all her time there, though. Sometimes she was allowed to stay at Manor Lodge in the deer park nearby. It cost George Talbot a lot of money to look after the rebel queen and her many servants.

After nearly fourteen years, she was allowed to leave but was caught plotting to murder Queen Elizabeth. Mary Queen of Scots was sentenced to death, and in 1587 she was beheaded!

Mary Queen of Scots often stayed at Manor Lodge. Parts of the lodge and Turret House are still there.

Little Mesters

Sheffield was a busy market town by now. Around the castle walls were narrow streets of houses and shops. Behind these were gardens, yards, pigsties, paddocks, and cutlery workshops known as smithies. The cutlery makers in the smithies were known as 'little mesters'.

George Talbot provided materials that the cutlery makers needed. He mined coal and ironstone from his land and had charcoal blast-furnaces and smithies built. He also brought better steel by ship from Spain. Best of all, he built waterwheels on the rivers to power the cutlers' grinding wheels. With water-power, grinders could sharpen more blades and do a better job.

By 1637 there were thirty-one cutler's wheels. Sheffield cutlers became well-known for their skills in making knives, scissors and tools. Many of them did not make forks though, as most people did not use them! By the late 1600s about three out of every five men were working in the cutlery trade.

The Shepherd Wheel has been at Whitely Woods since before 1584. It turned twenty grindstones.

In 1672, there were 224 smithies in Sheffield centre. That was almost half the houses!

Demolished!

In 1642, something happened that changed Sheffield forever. King Charles I was a stubborn ruler who tried to make religious changes many people did not want. He made his parliament angry and went to war against them!

In April 1643, the Duke of Newcastle and his Royalist army took control of Sheffield castle. Then, in August 1644, a parliamentary army arrived and attacked the castle. The local people wanted to help! Miners tried to dig a tunnel under the moat, while iron workers made cannonballs. The soldiers bombarded the castle with cannon for twenty-four hours! Then Colonel John Bright arrived with two bigger cannon. They soon broke through the wall. The Royalist soldiers surrendered!

King Charles lost the war, and parliament ordered Royalist castles to be destroyed. In 1648, Sheffield's great old castle was demolished. Many of the old stones were used for new buildings in the town.

People carried their own cutlery with them. It was often given as a Christening gift.

SPOT THIS!

The Old Queen's Head Inn on Pond Hill was named after Mary. It was built about 1475 as a banqueting hall. Can you spot the Queen?

CELT
500 BC

ROMAN
AD 43-410

ANGLO-
SAXON
AD 450-
1066

VIKING
AD 865-
1066

MEDIEV
TIME
1066
1485

In 1624, the Company of Cutlers in Hallamshire was formed. They kept a list of craftsmen and had rules to make sure cutlery and tools were made correctly. William is an imaginary character living in Sheffield. He tells us about his day as an apprentice cutlery-maker.

By 1614 there were 440 knife-makers, 31 shear- and sickle-makers and 27 scissor-makers in Sheffield and the surrounding villages.

RULES OF THE COMPANY OF CUTLERS IN HALLAMSHIRE 1624:

An apprentice must serve his master for a minimum of 7 years. During that time, he must not marry.

In return, the master must teach his apprentice, and provide him with lodging and food.

I want to be a little mester when I grow up, with my own workshop and apprentice!

Year of Our Lord 1670

Today was my first day at work! Father is training me to be a cutlery maker. He makes knives and pocket-knives. His smithy is in a brick lean-to at the back of our house. First he sent me off to fetch coal for the fire. That was the dull part! When the fire was ready, Father buried the end of a steel bar in it. Then he blasted it with air from his bellows. That helped it burn really hot! Once the steel was glowing, he brought it out and hammered it into a knife shape on his anvil. He cut off the knife, and plunged it into a stone trough of water to harden it. I wanted a try, but he wouldn't let me. I had to fetch more coal, and sweep the floor! Next we went to the riverside to grind some knives on a grindstone. It was dusty work, and made me cough. After that he gave me some knives to polish. I made them shiny and bright, and Father fitted the handles on. In seven years I can have my own smithy, then I won't have to sweep the floor and fetch the coal. My apprentice can do it!

Rows of knife-grinders sat on the saddle-seats of the water-powered grinding wheels at Shepherd Wheel.

Little Mester means a self-employed cutlery craftsman. 'Mester' was a Sheffield way of saying 'master'.

George Talbot did not like guarding Mary Queen of Scots. He was worried that she would escape!

How do we know?

Mary Queen of Scots and George Talbot wrote many letters which tell us about some of the things that happened. George Talbot complained that it was costing him a thousand pounds a year in plates and other things that were being spoiled and wasted by Mary's careless servants! In one letter, Mary Queen of Scots told a friend how to write secret letters to her in invisible ink. The message showed up when dipped in water!

By Tudor times, Sheffield already had a reputation for high quality cutlery.

In 1637, a man called John Harrison did a survey of the castle and all its lands in and around Hallamshire. He reported that 400 to 500 workmen were using the cutler's wheels on the rivers to grind their knives.

Many people wrote about the civil war. The Duke of Newcastle's wife, Mary Cavendish, wrote that the people of Sheffield were rebellious! Archaeologists found many things on the site of the old castle, including cannonballs.

From 1662 to 1689, the government made people pay tax for every fire hearth on their property. Records kept from 1672 tell us that 224 houses had smithies with hearths.

 15

A New Invention!

It is hot in the crucible workshop! The 'puller out' picks up his iron tongs and reaches down the melting hole to the underground furnace. He lifts out a glowing crucible and puts it down carefully. Then he takes off the lid. It is full of hot melted steel! The 'teemer' uses his tongs to pick up the heavy crucible. He leans his arm against his thigh to steady himself. Slowly and steadily he pours the melted steel into a mould. It runs out in a white stream and looks beautiful glowing in the gloomy workshop.

You can find the name 'Sheffield' or a maker's mark stamped on good cutlery.

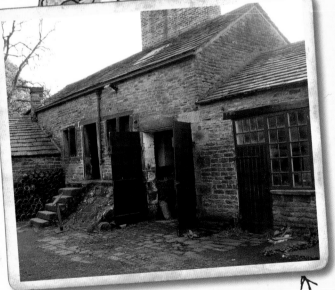

You can see a pile of crucibles stacked outside the old furnace room at Abbeydale Industrial Hamlet museum. They were used to make scythes and other tools.

Exciting Times

Georgian times brought exciting new inventions in Sheffield. A watchmaker called Benjamin Huntsman was unhappy with the steel he was using for clock springs. He did many experiments and in 1742 he found a way to make better steel in clay pots called crucibles. Soon everyone wanted to use his steel! Sheffield became known around the world for its steelmaking.

Around 1743, a cutlery maker called Thomas Boulsover made another discovery. While repairing a silver and copper knife handle, he heated it and the silver melted onto the copper. This gave him the idea to make copper buttons and knife handles with a thin layer of silver on top. It was called Old Sheffield Plate. Soon, other firms began using it to make candlesticks, teapots, jugs and bowls.

...1742 CRUCIBLE STEEL INVENTED...1743 OLD SHEFFIELD PLATE INVENTED...

Water and Steam Power

At this time, heavy goods were transported by packhorses or carts. It was very slow. But that was to change! In 1751, a canal was dug as far as Tinsley. In 1819, it was brought right to the town centre. Now, heavy loads could be easily moved by barges and large boats. It was a great success!

By 1770, there were about 133 water wheels, with between three and six on every mile of river! But more changes were on the way. In the 1780s, Sheffield's steel and iron producers began using steam-powered engines. Slowly they began to replace the water wheel.

The growing industries needed workers, so many people came from the countryside to work in Sheffield. In 1736, there were 10,121 people living in the town. By 1801 this had grown to 31,314! The Industrial Revolution was changing Sheffield!

3,500 leeches were used in the new dispensary in one year!

John R Watts Cutlery Works on Lambert Street was set up in 1765. The building still proudly advertises the goods made there.

Cholera!

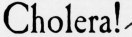

Poor families lived crowded together in small back-to-back houses. Out in the yard would be a water pump and toilet which they shared with neighbours. Sewage and waste water ran through open drains and got into the water supply. The streets were sometimes flooded with smelly water from the river. Sheffield was a grimy, smoky town with soot floating in the air. A lot of people had lung diseases.

Then, in July 1832, cholera struck! By November, the disease had killed 402 people in Sheffield. On the 2nd July that year, a new dispensary was opened in a house in Tudor Place to treat the sick poor. So many people came, it had to move to a bigger building. Some sick people were treated with blood-sucking leeches. It probably didn't help!

Cholera was spread by dirty drinking water, but no one knew that then.

A monument near Norfolk Park was built in memory of the people who died of cholera.

SPOT THIS!

Can you spot this bronze statue of steelmen at Meadowhall? Look for the rag in the steelman's mouth. It's to protect his lips from the heat!

Highwaymen!

A new kind of public transport came to Sheffield in 1760. The first stagecoach, pulled by six horses, began running from Sheffield to London. Then, in 1785, the first Royal Mail Coach service began delivering daily post. With stops along the way, the ride to London took 26 hours! It was a dangerous journey, as there were many thieves and highwaymen on the road.

Ten-year-old Richard lives in a cottage on Balm Green. In this imagined account he tells us about the day he went with his friends to see how a highwayman was punished. It's a grisly tale!

This model of the gibbet hangs outside the Noose and Gibbet Inn, Attercliffe.

There must have been at least 40,000 people come to see Spence Broughton's body!

Spence Broughton's bones were left hanging for nearly 36 years!

Monday 16th April, 1792

Everyone in Sheffield is gossiping about it! Spence Broughton's body is hanging from the gibbet on Attercliffe Common. It's his punishment for holding up the mail coach with John Oxley and stealing the mail! John Oxley got away but Spence Broughton was caught. He was hanged at Tyburn then taken to Attercliffe. Mother says it is a warning to boys who might want to be a highwayman. I went with my friends, Tom and John. We set off across Lady's Bridge and walked to Attercliffe Common. It only took us an hour or so. There was a great crowd of people on foot and on horseback, all going the same way. When we got there, we saw hundreds of people coming the other way from Rotherham. The Arrow Inn nearby was doing a roaring trade! George the innkeeper was at his wit's end trying to serve all the people shouting for ale! We squeezed through the crowd and saw Spence Broughton on the gibbet. Tom and John said they felt sorry for him and lots of other people did too. Some were singing songs about him! I don't think he should have stolen from the mail coach, but he didn't deserve to hang.

This memorial to Thomas Boulsover who lived from 1705 to 1788 stands on the spot where he discovered Sheffield plate.

A hallmark is stamped on silverware to show where it has come from. This one is from John R Watts.

The Norfolk knife has over seventy blades and took two years to make. It was made for the Great Exhibition of 1851 by Joseph Rodgers & Sons.

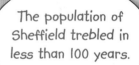

The population of Sheffield trebled in less than 100 years.

How do we know?

A writer called Daniel Defoe visited Sheffield and wrote about it in 1726. He tells us,

'The town of Sheffield is very populous and large, the streets narrow, and the houses dark and black, occasioned by the continued smoke of the forges, which are always at work.'

A Sheffield Board of Health was created to plan what to do about cholera. They kept records of their meetings, and how much money was spent on medicines and coffins. A list was made with the names of everyone who died. The dispensary kept records of how many leeches they used and how much they cost! Newspapers from the time can also tell us about the cholera outbreak. They printed reports of how many people died and how many recovered. We can also find out about Spence Broughton from newspapers, as well as from prison records.

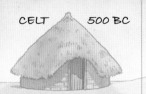
CELT   500 BC

ROMAN AD 43-410

ANGLO-SAXON AD 450-1066

VIKING AD 865-1066

MEDIEVAL TIME
1066-1485

Full Steam Ahead!

A girl and her little brother wave out of the window as the *Victory* slowly chugs its way out of the new station. Their parents are taking them to Rotherham on the first passenger train from Sheffield! A huge crowd has gathered to watch! Everyone cheers as the train passes by in a cloud of steam. It's an exciting day. Now people can catch a train from the centre of town, it will make travelling much easier and faster!

> 300 people rode on the first train from Sheffield to Rotherham!

A New Railway

Sheffield now began to change at an amazing speed, starting with a new railway station! The Wicker station opened on 31st October, 1838. The first passenger train ran the next day, pulled by a steam engine called *Victory*. It arrived in Rotherham 17 minutes later.

Enormous new steel works were built in the Lower Don Valley. Here they could use the railway to bring in coal and iron, and send out finished goods. In 1858, Henry Bessemer opened a steel works using his own invention, the Bessemer Converter. This could make huge amounts of steel very fast and looked like a volcano going off! It was used to make steel for railway tracks around the world. The biggest customer was America.

But Sheffield wasn't just known for steel. In 1842, George Bassett opened his sweet factory, providing jobs for many people. It became famous for making licorice allsorts!

This painting from 1854 shows us Sheffield was growing bigger, and more smoky!

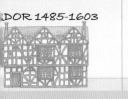

Children at Work!

Many children didn't go to school full time. Some were sent out to work at the age of 11! Boys worked in the steel works and often got burned. Many girls started work aged 14 as errand lasses helping the buffer girls. They learned the job by watching the buffer girls working the polishing machines. These buffed the steel cutlery and teapots to a shine. It was very dirty work and the buffer girls' hands often got scratched or burned. They wore brown paper aprons to soak up splashes of oil and protect their clothes.

The Great Sheffield Flood

By 1861, there were nearly 220,000 people in Sheffield. More water was needed, and new reservoirs were built. Then, on the night of 11th March 1864, disaster struck! After a stormy day, a great crack appeared in the new Dale Dyke Dam. The dam burst and water roared down the valley to Sheffield, sweeping away houses, mills, workshops, schools and bridges. Around 4,697 houses were flooded and at least 240 people drowned, but some had a lucky escape. One man kept his wife and six children safe by putting them all on a big bed where they floated until the flood water went down!

Flood damage at Ball Street.

In the 1860's, boys of seven or eight had jobs in the steelworks, working twelve hour shifts!

Most people did not have bathrooms. They had to wash in a tin bath in front of the fire!

Better Times

After the terrible flood, better times were ahead. A rich steelmaker called Mark Firth made a present of land to the town which became Firth Park. He also opened Firth College, which taught arts and science. Another steelmaker called Thomas Jessop paid for the Jessop Hospital for women. In 1873, the first horse trams began running, making it easier for people to go shopping and get to work.

Slowly, better drains and toilets were built. New pipes brought in clean water from the reservoirs. Swimming baths were built, which also had bathrooms. Now people could have a proper wash!

SPOT THIS!

This Bessemer Converter is at Kelham Island Industrial Museum. Can you spot where the molten steel pours out?

Robert is a boy who might have lived in Hillsborough. In this imaginary account he tells us about his job on the horse trams.

Sheffield is built on seven hills, so there's plenty of work for me and the horses.

Monday 5th May, 1890

I'm a tip lad, and that's a very important job! When the horse trams get to a steep hill, like Cemetery Road, they need an extra horse to help pull them up. That's where I'm needed! I'm in charge of the extra horse. When we've helped pull a tram to the top of the hill, it goes on its way, and I take the horse back down to wait for the next tram. At night, when it's gone dark, we light oil lamps on the tram, but they don't give much light.

One day, two horses were waiting to be harnessed to a tram, when we heard a bugle call from Hillsborough army barracks. Now these two horses used to belong to the army, so as soon as they heard the bugle, off they went! I ran after them and found them in the barracks yard. The soldiers were all laughing.

I start work at seven o'clock in the morning and work for fifteen hours. There's even a special tram at six o'clock for the workmen. I'm glad I don't work on that one. I like Sundays best because the trams don't start running until one o'clock. That means I can have a lie-in!

You can find out what it was like to ride on a horse tram like this one at Crich Tramway Village.

The first horse-drawn tramway opened in 1873 and ran between Lady's Bridge and Attercliffe.

Walker & Hall on Howard Street employed almost 2,000 workers.

Mark Firth gave Firth Park to the town in 1875. It was opened by Prince Edward and his wife Princess Alexandra.

How do we know?

In 1862 a report was made on working conditions for children in Sheffield. Children tell us in their own voices what their work was like. One boy tells how he often burned his hands, and once spent two months off work after getting a piece of steel through his thigh.

Town records show the efforts that were made to improve water supplies. Insurance claims tell us who died in the flood, and what buildings were damaged. A journalist called Samuel Harrison gathered together reports of what happened in the flood. Photos were also taken showing what the town looked like afterwards.

In 1872 a Sheffield newspaper wrote a report about the state of the town. It tells us that children played in the filthy streets in puddle holes. The streets were covered in smelly mud that got trailed into houses making them impossible to keep clean.

In the 1800s Sheffield was growing bigger, and more smoky!

CELT
500 BC

ROMAN
AD 43-410

ANGLO-
SAXON
AD 450-
1066

VIKING
AD 865-
1066

MEDIEV
TIMES
1066-
1485

Attack from Above!

A siren wails and the children dash for the air raid shelter in the garden. It's too dark to see and they stumble across the muddy ground. They can already hear the drone of German planes in the sky, coming to drop their bombs. It's a different sound from the friendly British Spitfires they often see fly over. They reach the shelter and their mother pulls the door shut behind them. It's cold in the shelter, and they all shiver. Will their house still be there in the morning?

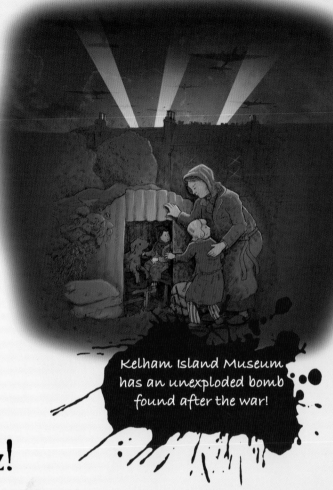

The German code name for the bomb attack on Sheffield was 'Crucible'.

Kelham Island Museum has an unexploded bomb found after the war!

Blitz!

In 1939, World War Two broke out. Cutlery and teapot factories switched to making tools and weapons. A lot of the men went to fight in the war and women took over their jobs in the factories. Even when the air raid sirens went, many women bravely carried on working. Their work was too important to leave!

The worst attack came on the night of 12th December, 1940 when 336 German aircraft flew over, dropping bombs for about nine hours. Many buildings were damaged, and much of the town centre was destroyed. More bombers came back three days later, and attacked the factories, but only a few were badly damaged. Altogether, 589 people were killed.

Some people took shelter in cellars during the air raids. But many families had moved into new houses between the wars and did not have cellars. They had to spend the night in Anderson shelters in their gardens.

Children from Sheffield were evacuated to live with families in the countryside where it was safer from bombing raids.

...1913 STAINLESS STEEL INVENTED...1939-1945 WORLD WAR TWO...

TUDOR
1485-1603

STUART
1603-1714

GEORGIAN
1714-1837

VICTORIAN
1837-1901

MODERN
TIMES
1902-NOW

A New Kind of Steel

All through the 1900s, steelmakers were looking for ways of improving steel. One problem was that it kept going rusty! Around 1913 a Sheffield man called Harry Brearley discovered a way to make steel that wouldn't go rusty. It was called stainless steel and was used for making submarines, aircraft and warships.

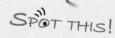

This mighty steam hammer, used for pressing steel, can be seen by the side of the road at Brightside.

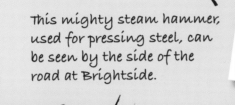

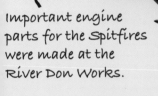

Important engine parts for the Spitfires were made at the River Don Works.

Rebuilding

After the war, new shops and houses were built and important old buildings were washed. The Clean Air Act in 1956 meant that smokeless fuel had to be used in houses and factories.

Slowly, other countries began making more cutlery, tools and steel at lower prices. There was less work for Sheffield factories and, by the 1980s, many were closed. In 1990, the huge Meadowhall shopping mall was built where factories used to be. Big new sports centres and an Arena were built. These brought new jobs for many people!

Many changes have happened, but there are still reminders around Sheffield of its proud steel industry. Special steels are still made here but there are no more smelly chimneys. Smoky Sheffield is a thing of the past!

In wartime, Sheffield women worked in the factories. They became known as the Women of Steel.

SPOT THIS!

Look out for the clock tower in Orchard Square. Every 15 minutes, statues of a grinder and a buffer girl pop out.

CELT
500 BC

ROMAN
AD 43-410

ANGLO-
SAXON
AD 450-
1066

VIKING
AD 865-
1066

MEDIEV
TIME
1066
1485

Alice is a ten-year-old girl who might have lived in Sheffield during World War Two. In this imaginary letter to her cousin, Alice tells her story of the night of the Blitz.

I'd rather face the bombs with Mum than be sent away to live with strangers.

Friday 13th December, 1940

About seven o'clock last night, the air raid sirens started wailing! I grabbed my gas mask, cardigan and coat and went in the Anderson shelter. It was damp and cold, and there were snails and worms! Our cat Ginger ran in and jumped on my knee. Dad's an air raid warden, so he dashed off to make sure everyone was in a shelter. Mum made a jug of hot cocoa and hurried to our shelter, just in time! The next minute, we heard German bombers droning overhead and the thud of bombs falling! I could feel the ground shaking! We couldn't sleep for all the loud bangs, so we huddled under quilts and played Ludo by candlelight. It was nine hours before we heard the all clear siren. When we went outside, the sky was lit up orange and red with fires, and the air was full of black smoke. Our house windows had all been blown in! When Dad came home he told us a lot of schools, houses, shops and cinemas had been bombed. But he said the new Rex cinema is all right, so we'll be able to see the new Laurel and Hardy film. That cheered me up.

Knitting wool was found in the rubble cleared from a shop. It was collected and knitted into jumpers and balaclavas!

When the bombing raids started, the cinemas closed. But they soon opened again to boost morale.

**REX CINEMA
NOW OPEN**

PATHÉ NEWS
MATINEE SCREENING
SATURDAY MORNING
SERIALS

Sheffield trams have changed quite a lot since the days of horse trams!

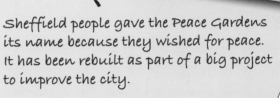

Sheffield people gave the Peace Gardens its name because they wished for peace. It has been rebuilt as part of a big project to improve the city.

Today, over 500,000 people live in Sheffield.

How do we know?

From 1900, cameras were more widely available and easier to use. There are many photos that show women at work in the factories, children being evacuated during the war and bomb-damaged buildings after the Blitz. Some of the damaged buildings are still there. You can still see where the Wicker Arches and City Hall have been repaired after being damaged by bombs.

Many people who lived through the war wrote down what happened in books, letters or diaries. Since then, some have also recorded their memories on film or told their stories on the Internet. Newspaper reports can also tell us what happened.

Some people have kept their old Anderson shelters to use as garden sheds.

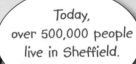

CELT
500 BC

ROMAN
AD 43-410

ANGLO-
SAXON
AD 450-
1066

VIKING
AD 865-
1066

MEDIE
TIME
106(
148.

Sheffield Today and Tomorrow

Sheffield first grew into a town under the protection of its great castle. The castle lords helped to build the industries that made it grow until it became the City of Sheffield in 1893. People like Floriana, William, Richard, Robert and Alice survived through difficult and dangerous times to make the city the successful place it is today. Many people call it Steel City, and now you know why!

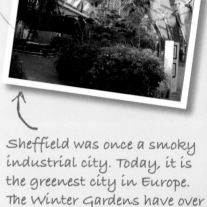

Sheaf Square is the gateway to the city for anyone arriving by train. It has a stunning stainless steel sculpture called Cutting Edge, a reminder of the city's history.

Sheffield was once a smoky industrial city. Today, it is the greenest city in Europe. The Winter Gardens have over 2,500 plants from around the world.

You can feel proud to be a part of Sheffield's future.

At the Millennium Gallery you can see arts and crafts old and new, and find out how cutlery was made. Look out for the amazing sculpture made of cutlery by Johnny White called Barking up the Wrong Tree.

In 1991, Helen Sharman became the first British person in space. Not every city has their very own astronaut!

...1994 SUPERTRAM BEGINS RUNNING...

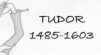

Sheffield Wednesday Football club was formed in 1867. Their stadium was once at Owlerton, which is where they got the nickname 'The Owls'!

Sheffield United Football Club was formed in 1889. They are nicknamed 'The Blades' because of Sheffield's great steel industry.

Sheffield FC is the world's oldest football club, founded in 1857.

Sheffield University was founded in 1905. Mark Firth's Arts and Science college became part of it.

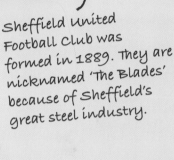

How will they know?

Future people will have many ways to see what Sheffield is like today. The Internet is a constantly growing record of life today. Important things are preserved in museums for future people to see. Special buildings like the Cathedral and Abbeydale Industrial Hamlet are now protected to prevent them being knocked down or changed. Can you think of any special buildings that you think should be protected?

Many well-known actors appear in plays and pantomimes at The Crucible Theatre. It is also famous for being home to the World Snooker Championships!

Glossary

AD – a short way of writing the Latin words anno Domini, which mean 'in the year of our Lord', i.e. after the birth of Christ.

Air raid – during World War Two, enemy planes dropped bombs on Britain. This was an air raid. To warn people the planes were coming, sirens wailed out all over the city.

Anderson shelter – a concrete shelter buried in your garden, where you could go for protection when bombs fell during World War Two.

Apprentice – boys could start to learn a trade when they were 12. While they were learning they were called an apprentice.

Archaeologist – a person who studies the past by examining buildings and objects left behind by previous people and cultures.

Blitz – when Germans bombed towns during World War Two, it was called the Blitz.

Charter – written permission to do something. A Royal Charter, means that the king or queen has given permission.

Cholera – a deadly disease caused by filthy water.

Civil war – a war in which the people of a country fight each other.

Cohort – a band of soldiers in the Roman Legion.

Domesday Book – William the Conqueror sent his men all over England to check how much land and wealth his kingdom had and who owned it. The results were written in a book called the Domesday Book, which survives to this day.

Evacuate – to leave your home and live somewhere else for safety.

Fort or fortress – a large, strong building offering military support and protection.

Furnace – a very big oven, used for burning rubbish or melting metals.

Gas mask – used in World War Two, this mask protected you from breathing poisonous gas.

Gibbet – a wooden structure from which criminals used to be hanged.

Granary – a building or room where grain was stored to keep it dry.

Highwayman – a masked robber who waited on roads (highways) to steal from travellers.

Knead – to push and pull dough to make sure the ingredients are mixed.

Moat – a deep trench, filled with water, that surrounds a fortress or castle.

Monastery – a place where monks live and worship.

Monk – a male member of a religious community.

Parliamentarian – anyone who fought on the side of Oliver Cromwell and Parliament in the English Civil War. Also known as a Roundhead.

Quernstone – another name for a millstone, a small circular stone used for grinding corn.

Ramparts – raised walls or walkway surrounding a fort.

Reservoir – a large area of land used to hold drinking water.

Royalist – anyone who fought on the side of King Charles I in the English Civil War. Also known as a Cavalier.

Venison – meat from deer.

Index

Acknowledgements

The author and publishers would like to thank the following people for their generous help:
the staff at Sheffield Local Studies Library; the staff at Museums Sheffield.

The publishers would like to thank the following people and organizations
for their permission to reproduce material on the following pages:
p6: Betacam–SP/Shutterstock; p7: MatthiasKabel/Wikipedia; p9: Paul Walker/Flickr; Ella S. Armitage;
p13: Sheffield City Council; p14: ArcHeritage and Sheffield City Council; p15: Shutterstock;
p16: Abbeydale_Industrial_Hamlet-Warofdreams_wikipedia;
p19: copyright Herbert Housley MBE; p20: Sheffield City Council;
p21: Mike Armitage ts-Chemical Engineer/Wikipedia; p22–24: Sheffield City Council;
p25: Paul Drabot/Shutterstock; Steve Butler; p28: Johnny White, Barking Up the Right Tree,
2000/Museums Sheffield: Millennium Gallery; Alan Saunders (Kaptain Kobold)/Wikipedia

All other images copyright of Hometown World

Written by Ann Wright
Educational consultant: Neil Thompson
Local history consultant: Anne McQueen
Designed by Stephen Prosser

Illustrated by Kate Davies, Dynamo Ltd, Virginia Gray, Tim Hutchinson,
Peter Kent, Nick, Shewring, Tim Sutcliffe
Additional photographs by Alex Long, Ann Wright

First published by HOMETOWN WORLD in 2011
Hometown World Ltd
7 Northumberland Buildings
Bath BA1 2JB

www.hometownworld.co.uk

Copyright © Hometown World Ltd 2011

ISBN 978-1-84993-004-8

CELT	ROMAN	ANGLO-SAXON	VIKING	MEDIEVAL TIMES
500 BC	AD 43-410	AD 450-1066	AD 865-1066	1066-1485